# SUGAR ART
## *Ideas*

# SWEETS &
# TREATS

# SUGAR ART
## *Ideas*

# SWEETS & TREATS

## LINDSAY JOHN BRADSHAW

Series Editor: ALISON LEACH

MEREHURST PRESS
—— LONDON ——

Published 1989 by Merehurst Press
Ferry House, 51-57 Lacy Road, Putney
London SW15 1PR

Co-published in Australia and New Zealand by Child & Associates,
Unit C, 5 Skyline Place, Frenchs Forest, 2086, Australia.

ISBN 1 85391 048 1

Managing Editor: Alison Leach
Designer: Richard Slater
Photographer: Graham Tann, assisted by Alister Thorpe, Lucy Baker and
Gary Taylor
Typeset by Vision Typesetting, Manchester
Colour separation by Scantrans Pte Limited, Singapore
Printed in Belgium by Proost International Book Production

ACKNOWLEDGEMENTS
The Publishers would like to thank the following for their help and advice:
Julia Catchpole of C.E.P. Chocolate & Sugar Moulds, 7 Durrington Road,
Bournemouth BH7 6PU
B. R. Mathews & Son, 12 Gipsy Hill, Upper Norwood, London SE19 1NN
David Mellor, 26 James Street, Covent Garden, London WC2E 8PA
Keylink Limited, Blackburn Road, Rotherham S61 2DR
Wheatsheaf Graphics, 50 Grays Inn Road, London WC1X 8LT

**Warning**
Cocktail sticks and wired flowers must only be used for display purposes in sugarcraft. Great care
should always be taken to ensure there is no possibility of any particles being eaten accidentally.

Important: use only one set of measurements. The quantities
given in metric are not always exact conversions of the
imperial measurements. Cup conversions of imperial
measurements are given below.

| Imperial | Cups |
|---|---|
| 5 fl oz liquid | $\frac{2}{3}$ cup |
| 10 fl oz liquid | $1\frac{1}{4}$ cups |
| 20 fl oz liquid | $2\frac{1}{2}$ cups |
| 40 fl oz liquid | 5 cups |
| 1 lb granulated or caster (superfine) sugar | 2 cups |
| 1 lb brown sugar | 2 cups |
| 1 lb icing (confectioner's) sugar | $3\frac{1}{2}$ cups |
| 1 lb butter | 2 cups |
| 1 lb dried fruit | 3 cups |
| 1 lb flour | 4 cups |
| 8 oz glacé cherries | 1 cup |
| 4 oz chopped nuts | 1 cup |
| 4 oz cocoa powder | 1 cup |
| 1 oz flour | $\frac{1}{4}$ cup |
| 1 oz granulated or caster (superfine) sugar | 2 tablespoons |
| 1 oz butter | 2 tablespoons |

# CONTENTS

Foreword    7

Introduction    8

Ingredients    10

Moulds    12

Peppermint alphabets    14

Creamy fudge    16

Ginger and hazelnut treats    18

Rum and raisin snowballs    20

Marzipan chestnuts    22

Candied pineapple    24

Caramel glazed fruits    24

Crystallized flowers    26

Quick decorated chocolates    28

Chocolate liqueurs    30

Cherry whirls    32

Pineapple kirsch creams    34

Cherry brandy cups    36

Coffee and walnut supremes    38

Special truffles    40

Alpine brandy log    42

Ginger Christmas tree decorations    44

Florentines    46

Cake truffles    48

Fancy cakes    50

Fruity crunchies    52

Little Christmas puddings    54

Crispy choirboys    56

Lolly faces    58

Shortbread settings    60

Presentation and packaging    62

Piped chocolate decorations    64

# FOREWORD

I feel privileged to have been asked to write the foreword for SWEETS AND TREATS, the latest book by Lindsay John Bradshaw.

This book is unique since it not only gives the decorator superb instructions on how to make the sweets and chocolates but it also places special emphasis on the decoration and presentation of these goods. Lindsay leaves nothing out and his book covers all aspects of this delightful art. It is so attractively presented that everyone who reads it will wish to go ahead and follow the ideas.

I am sure that one of the main attractions will be that this book is the work of one of our country's top craftsmen, of whom we can be proud. I have known Lindsay since he started teaching some eight years ago and have always admired both his brilliant artistic skills and his natural ability when teaching and demonstrating to challenge and inspire the novice and advanced student alike.

As well as being a Lecturer in Cake Design and Decoration at the Salford College of Technology, Lindsay has recently been appointed Editor of *British Sugarcraft News*: his many skills and hard work in this capacity are very much admired and appreciated.

I know that this book will fill a void in the literature on sugarcraft. I wish Lindsay the success with it that he well deserves.

**June E. Elwood**, M.Inst.B.B., M.C.F.A.(C.G.)
Principal, The June Elwood Cake Artistry Studio, Manchester
Founder member, The British Sugarcraft Guild

# INTRODUCTION

With sugar art becoming more and more popular, the need for new ideas has increased equally. In this series each book covers a specialized area of cake or confectionery decoration, combining numerous original ideas with a few old favourites executed with a new approach.

The emphasis throughout is on design and decoration, offering the discerning cake decorator a range of colourful and attractively decorated sweets and treats.

Many of the sugarcraft techniques will probably already be familiar to you, making sweets and treats an easy extension from your existing cake decorating interests – one that may even take over from your royal icing or sugarpaste work!

Flavour and texture are all important in sweets and treats, so it is essential not to substitute cheaper ingredients. The recipes developed especially for this book do not skimp on quality in any way. The combination of the best available ingredients, professional production techniques and imaginative decoration, both classic and modern, will enable you to achieve results of a very high standard.

Many of the recipes require the minimum amount of equipment, although some call for more specialized items to give a more professional finish.

I hope you will enjoy making the sweets and treats described in this book. Don't eat too many while you are preparing them – save some for your friends so that they too can experience both the delicious flavourings and your artistic skills!

**Lindsay John Bradshaw**

# INGREDIENTS

Most of the tools and equipment used for making sweets and treats are ordinary kitchen or household items. The more unusual items are available from cake decorating shops and specialist sugarcraft suppliers.

## Choice of ingredients

To make delicious sweets and treats good quality ingredients are essential. When choosing ingredients from nuts and dried fruits to chocolate and liqueurs, always buy the best available. It is much better to pay a little bit more so that the end products taste really good.

## Chocolate

The two main types of chocolate used in sugarcraft are baker's chocolate and couverture.

Baker's chocolate is sometimes referred to as a covering. As it does not require any special preparation, it is far easier to work with than couverture. Baker's chocolate does not have as good a flavour as its far superior counterpart. Couverture is often called 'the real thing' because of its excellent flavour and smoothness. It is more expensive and needs tempering before it can be used.

All the recipes in this book requiring chocolate can be made with either baker's or couverture – the choice is yours – but for really special items like the truffles and chocolate liqueurs, the extra cost of using couverture is justified as it marries well with the flavourings and spirits used in the recipes.

Baker's chocolate is available from all sugarcraft suppliers and most large supermarkets. It can be bought in slabs or in the form of buttons. The main difference from couverture is that most of the cocoa butter has been removed and been replaced with a vegetable fat, eliminating the need for tempering and also producing a softer-cutting set.

Use a double jacketed saucepan to melt the chocolate over hot but not boiling water. Heat to 38–43°C (100–110°F) or until smooth with no lumps. Take care not to overheat the chocolate (particularly important if not using a thermometer) as otherwise fat bloom (white streaks) may appear. Never allow steam to get into the chocolate. Baker's chocolate can be refrigerated to quicken the contraction if using moulds.

Sweets made with couverture will have a far superior gloss, more smoothness to the palate and an outstandingly better flavour. You can purchase couverture from specialist sugarcraft suppliers and bakery sundriesmen. Do not substitute bars of dessert chocolate as these are not pure couverture.

Tempering the chocolate involves heating and then cooling it to various specified temperatures so that the cocoa butter crystallizes to produce a high gloss and good 'snap' when set. A sugar thermometer is essential for accuracy.

Chop the chocolate into small pieces and place in a double jacketed saucepan over simmering, *not* boiling water. When the chocolate reaches 46°C (115°F), remove the pan from the jacket and heat and place in a bowl or sink of cold water. Stir the chocolate until it cools to 27–28°C (80–82°F). Return the pan to the jacket and heat to 31°C (88°F). The chocolate is now tempered and ready for use.

For tempering milk chocolate the temperatures should be 1°C (2°F) lower at *all* stages.

The procedure for tempering white couverture is similar but refer to the manufacturers' specifications for recommended temperatures.

Incorrectly tempered couverture will not set as it should and it will be difficult to release the chocolate from the moulds. White or grey bloom may also be visible.

## Ganache

Several of the recipes in this book refer to a ganache base. Ganache is a rich cream and chocolate mixture which can be piped, spread, poured or moulded. It is a most versatile medium and well worth making for its flavour and smoothness. Milk, plain or white chocolate can be used and the ganache can be flavoured to make numerous delicious variations.

## Flavourings

Most of the flavourings mentioned in this book are the real products. If you replace these with essences, you will reduce the cost considerably but equally you will reduce the quality of the flavourings. The main flavourings used in the book are rum, brandy, kirsch, maraschino and such liqueurs as Grand Marnier and Tia Maria. The only essences used are vanilla and almond.

## Fillings

All the fillings demand quality, freshness and good flavour. Use butter and double (thick) dairy cream where stated. Fresh nuts and fruits are readily available at supermarkets, where many different varieties are prepacked.

# MOULDS

A moulded chocolate shell is the basis of many of the sweets and treats in this book. To avoid repeating the procedure in each recipe, the details are fully explained here, with cross-references where necessary.

A selection of commercially available chocolate moulds can be purchased from sugarcraft suppliers. Provided you look after the moulds during and after use, they should give you years of service. The flexible, clear plastic type are quite inexpensive while the sturdier and probably more serviceable, brown-coloured plastic moulds can be up to six times more expensive.

## Making moulded chocolates

First ensure that your mould is spotless. Use clean cotton wool to polish inside each shape carefully, including all the crevices and corners. This will ensure that you achieve a better gloss on your chocolate work.

Prepare your baker's chocolate or couverture as described above, taking care to adhere to the recommended temperatures and procedures.

Pour or pipe chocolate into the shapes, filling to the top edge. Tap the tray gently to remove any air bubbles, then leave to start setting. Fill a second tray of moulds while the first is setting.

Check the moulds frequently at regular intervals to see if the chocolate is setting around the edges. As soon as it is, turn the tray upside down over your chocolate pan and drain off the excess chocolate.

Use a small palette knife to clean off any remaining chocolate and then place the tray upside down to let the chocolate finish setting. This will make a small rim form around the inside edge which is ideal to work to when sealing the base of the chocolates. If you do not like the idea of a rim on the inside edge, simply leave the tray the other way up to finish setting.

The chocolate cases are now ready for the fillings. They can then be topped with a thin layer of chocolate to seal in the filling. When filled and sealed, the chocolates can be removed from the moulds by a gentle pressure and with the flexible kind by a little turning of the mould – being careful not to break it.

## Cleaning

After use wash the moulds in hot water using a mild detergent, rinse well and allow to drain. Dry the moulds with a soft clean cloth. Polish them with cotton wool (do this again when you use the mould next time) and pack between layers of soft tissue paper until required again.

## Hand-moulded chocolates

To save the expense of purchasing moulds, some recipes for hand-moulded chocolates are also included in this book. This method of sweet-making can be just as successful as using plastic pre-shaped moulds. Hand-moulding involves rolling and cutting shapes, and forming balls, ovals or fingers from the various pastes and mixtures.

# PEPPERMINT ALPHABETS

**Ingredients**
royal icing
egg white
assorted food colourings
box of peppermint cream
   chocolates

1 Prepare some run-icing for the run-out alphabet letters. Place some freshly made royal icing in a small bowl and add a small amount of unbeaten egg white (water can be used, if preferred), mixing thoroughly with a spoon. Do *not* beat the icing. This would create unwanted air bubbles that would spoil the appearance of your run-out work.

Add sufficient egg white to make a thick creamy consistency. When the spoon is lifted up and a ribbon of icing made across the mixture, the icing should find its own level after a count of about ten. Colour the icing as required. You can make the letters all the same colour or each one different, in which case you will need several small greaseproof paper piping bags, each containing a different colour of run-icing.

2 Make a tracing of the letters, either the full alphabet or just those needed for your chosen name or greeting. Place a piece of waxed paper over the tracing and outline the letters in royal icing and a No1 nozzle. For the outlines you can either use the same colour of icing as the one being used to flood-in or a contrasting colour which looks very effective.

After outlining the letters use scissors to cut a small hole at the end of the piping bag containing the run-icing. The hole should not be bigger than the size of a No2 nozzle. Flood-in the letters carefully and neatly, using a paint brush to assist the flow of the icing. Leave to dry in a gentle heat such as under a desk lamp.

When dry, carefully peel off the letters from the waxed paper, taking care not to damage any of them.

3 Using a little royal icing or melted chocolate, attach a run-out letter to each peppermint cream chocolate. If using royal icing, it is a good idea to colour the icing brown; if any should seep out beneath the letters, it will not be quite as noticeable as white icing would.

Arrange the letters in a fancy box to spell out the name or greeting and finish with a ribbon and bow. A full alphabet of letters packed in a gift box is a novel idea for a youngster who will find this way of learning the alphabet both interesting and delicious.

14

ABCDEF
GHIJKL
MNOPQ
RSTUVW
XYZ 123
4567890

# CREAMY FUDGE

**Ingredients**
125ml (4 fl oz) milk
125ml (4 fl oz) evaporated milk
575g (1¼lb) granulated sugar
125g (4oz) butter
5ml (1 tsp) vanilla essence
melted chocolate for dipping
  (*see page 10*)

1 Using a heavy-based saucepan, boil the milk, evaporated milk and sugar. Then add the butter and continue cooking to 115°C (250°F) – soft ball on a sugar thermometer. Stir the mixture occasionally. Remove from the heat and stir in the vanilla essence.
  To achieve a grainy-textured fudge, beat the mixture with a wooden spoon until it becomes thick. For a softer texture, let the mixture cool a little before beating.

2 Pour the mixture into a waxed paper-lined baking tray, about 17.5 × 20-cm (7 × 8-in), or into two of the sweet trays described on page 12. Lightly grease the waxed paper with a little butter. Leave the mixture to set for about 12 hours.
  Turn the mixture out of the tray in one piece and cut neatly into bite-sized pieces. The fudge can be left as it is or further decorated.

3 The fudge pieces may be dipped in melted milk or plain chocolate either completely or just up to the top edge as shown. Alternatively, you may like to add just a small amount of chocolate decoration in the form of a few lines of spun chocolate as described on page 52.
  You can add various nuts, fruits and flavourings to make a selection of different varieties. The quantities given below are for this recipe but you could, for example, easily divide your cooked fudge in two and add half these amounts just before you pour the fudge into the tray to set.
CHOCOLATE FUDGE    Add 30 g (2ml) sieved cocoa powder
CHERRY AND WALNUT FUDGE    Add 15ml (1 tbsp) each of chopped glacé cherries and chopped walnuts with a few drops of almond essence to taste
RUM AND RAISIN FUDGE    Add 50g (2oz) raisins which have been soaked in rum for a few hours

# GINGER AND HAZELNUT TREATS

## Ingredients

225g (8oz) marzipan
5ml 1 tsp) honey
25g (1oz) glacé ginger
25g (1oz) hazelnuts, finely
    chopped and lightly toasted
icing (confectioner's) sugar for
    dusting
melted chocolate for dipping
    (*see page 10*)
pouring fondant
green food colouring

**1** Knead the marzipan lightly to make it pliable, warming it slightly if necessary. Add the honey, ginger and hazelnuts and continue mixing until all the ingredients are evenly distributed. Use a little icing sugar to prevent the mixture from sticking to the work surface.

Roll out the mixture, dusting with a little icing sugar, into a long roll about 22-mm ($\frac{7}{8}$-in) diameter.

Cover a cake board with waxed paper. Cut the marzipan; roll into evenly sized pieces about 12-mm ($\frac{1}{2}$-in) thick. Place each piece on the prepared cake board, carefully neatening each one. Leave the pieces for a few hours to become firm before dipping.

**2** Prepare the chocolate by melting it gently in a double jacketed pan. Using a dipping fork or metal skewer, pick each piece of marzipan up and submerge in the melted chocolate up to the top edge, lift out and allow any excess chocolate to drain away, smoothing the base of the sweet along the edge of the pan or with a small palette knife. Place the sweets on waxed paper and leave to set.

**3** Prepare a small amount of pouring fondant to a relatively firm consistency (not too runny) suitable for piping drops. Use a double jacketed pan to heat the fondant to about 37°C (99°F), adjusting the consistency with water or sugar syrup. Colour the fondant pale green. Place a small amount in a greaseproof paper piping bag and snip off the end with scissors to make an opening about the size of a No2 nozzle. Pipe neat drops of fondant on to each sweet to fill the top surface. Leave to set.

# RUM AND RAISIN SNOWBALLS

**Ingredients**
50g (2oz) raisins
30ml (1 fl oz) rum
225g (8oz) marzipan
green food colouring
royal icing containing glycerine
icing (confectioner's) sugar for
    dusting

1 Place the raisins in a
    suitable air-tight plastic
container or clean jam jar with
screw-topped lid. Pour the rum
over the fruit, replace the lid
and turn gently to mix. Leave
to marinate for about 12 hours,
turning the container
occasionally.
    Colour the marzipan green
and roll out, using a little icing
sugar for dusting. Cut out
small circles of marzipan.

2 Lay a circle of marzipan in
    the palm of your hand and
indent a cupped shape with
your thumb.
    Place three or four rum-
soaked raisins (drain a little if
necessary) in the shaped
marzipan.
    Bring all the edges of the
marzipan together gently to
form a ball. Lightly roll to
retain the ball shape and leave
for a few hours to become
firm.

3 Scoop a little royal icing
    (with glycerine) into the
palm of both hands and gently
roll each marzipan ball, leaving
a peaked surface to resemble
snow. Place on waxed paper
and leave the icing to firm a
little. Lightly re-roll in royal
icing again if necessary to
cover completely. Place in
paper cases ready for
presentation.

# MARZIPAN CHESTNUTS

## Ingredients

marzipan
brown paste food colouring
green paste food colouring
orange paste food colouring
icing (confectioner's) sugar for
    dusting
egg white
royal icing
marzipan varnish

1 Colour half the marzipan dark brown and half dark green using paste food colourings and a little icing sugar to prevent the marzipan sticking to the work surface.

Make the centres of the chestnuts by rolling small balls of the brown-coloured marzipan. Place these on waxed paper and leave for a few hours to become firm. Alternatively, small chocolate truffles could be used for the centres.

2 Roll out the green-coloured marzipan to 3-mm ($\frac{1}{8}$-in) thickness and cut out circles large enough to enclose the chestnut centres. Wrap each chestnut centre in a green-coloured circle enclosing it completely. A little egg white may be required to stick the marzipan but do not use too much or the next step of removing a segment of marzipan may be difficult. Roll with gentle pressure to form neat balls.

Using a small sharp knife cut away a segment as shown and mark the remaining segments using a modelling tool or the back of a small knife.

Pipe on the spikes in royal icing using a No2 nozzle and pulling out to a sharp point.

3 To create the realistic colouring of the nut casings, first tint with pale green colouring and then with orange, avoiding the brown centre portion. Either spray the colour with an airbrush or apply edible petal dust with a dry brush.

Glaze the brown-coloured centres with marzipan varnish.

# CANDIED PINEAPPLE

**Ingredients**
225g (8oz) canned pineapple
   rings
175g (6oz) granulated sugar
5ml (1 tsp) lemon juice

1 Drain the juice from the pineapple rings, setting the fruit aside. Make up the fruit juice to 300ml (10 fl oz) with water and pour into a saucepan. Add the sugar and lemon juice and heat until a syrup is produced. Add the pineapple rings and bring to the boil. Remove from the heat and set aside for 24 hours.

2 On the next day re-boil the syrup and fruit mixture, remove from the heat and set aside again for 24 hours. Repeat this process until the fruit and syrup have been boiled a total of seven times. Drain off the resulting cold syrup and use to brush cake bases or as a stock syrup for fondant and glacé icing reduction.

3 Place the pineapple rings on a wire rack until dry enough to handle, when they should be stored between sheets of waxed paper ready for use. The candied pineapple may be cut into small wedge-shaped segments and placed in an attractive gift box lined with waxed paper to prevent the fruit sticking. Candied pineapple makes an ideal gift for someone to use as confectionery decorations or just simply to eat and enjoy!

# CARAMEL GLAZED FRUITS

**Ingredients**
a selection of fruits:
   cherries
   green and black grapes
   firm, just ripe strawberries
   mandarins
225g (8oz) granulated
   (superfine) sugar, warmed
60ml (4 tbsp) water
pinch of cream of tartar

1 Wash the cherries and grapes, leave to drain and dry on absorbent kitchen paper. Check over the strawberries for any blemished fruit, carefully wiping with a clean moist cloth and leaving the stalks on the berries. Peel the mandarins and separate the segments.

2 Make the glaze by placing the warmed sugar and water in a heavy-based saucepan and warming over a low heat until dissolved. Add the cream of tartar and boil the mixture. Use a pastry brush dipped into cold water to brush down the inside of the pan frequently to prevent crystallization. Do not stir the mixture. Continue boiling until the caramel becomes a very light golden colour when it is ready for use. Remove from the heat.

3 Dip the prepared fruit in the caramel, either holding the fruit by the stalk or picking it up with a wooden cocktail stick (toothpick). Place the dipped fruits on a lightly greased baking tray and leave until set. Present in small paper cases. Serve the fruits within 3–4 hours.

# CRYSTALLIZED FLOWERS

**Ingredients**
1 fresh rose
small bunch of fresh violets
2–3 stems of fresh freesias
gum arabic
colourless spirit such as gin or
    vodka
caster (superfine) sugar

1 Ideally use flowers from your garden or a friend's garden rather than commercially grown flowers that may have been sprayed with insecticides. Check that the flowers are clean and then carefully remove the petals, placing these on a piece of absorbent kitchen paper. Discard any petals that are in any way damaged or blemished.

Prepare a solution of gum arabic dissolved in a little colourless spirit and also a small dish or tray of caster sugar.

2 Using a clean paint brush or small pastry brush, brush each petal with the gum arabic solution and then lay on the caster sugar. Sprinkle sugar lightly over each petal – try if possible not to bruise the petals but ensure they are fully coated with sugar.

Place the sugared petals on a wire rack to allow air to circulate around them so that they dry quicker.

3 When dry, carefully remove from the wire rack and use as required to decorate sweets and treats such as Cherry Whirls (*see page 32*) or for your favourite soufflé, cheesecake or sherry trifle. If the petals are to be stored for later use, keep them in an air-tight jar. An attractive box filled with crystallized petals would make a welcome gift for an enthusiastic cook or sugarcraft artist for them to use on their own creations.

A different and less expensive way of crystallizing petals is to use egg white instead of the gum arabic solution. The petals will not, however, dry ready for use as quickly as the ones treated with spirit which evaporates quite rapidly.

# QUICK DECORATED CHOCOLATES

This is a novel way to personalize a box of commercially made chocolates. You could of course use your own home-made chocolates.

**Ingredients**
box of assorted chocolates
royal icing
assorted paste food colourings
pouring fondant

1 Remove the chocolates from the box and sort into similar shapes.

Using assorted paste food colourings, mix various bright colours of royal icing. Half-fill greaseproof paper piping bags with the different icings, using a No1 or No0 nozzle. To help to make the royal icing stick to the chocolate a little better and avoid the risk of it flaking off, add a small amount of slightly warmed pouring fondant to the royal icing.

2 Using the patterns provided, pipe the floral motifs and stems and leaves on to the chocolates.

Names can also be piped on with very tiny lettering.

3 Place the finished chocolates in paper or foil cases.

Instead of replacing the chocolates in their original box, use an attractive gift box with a ribbon and gift tag to make a really special individual present.

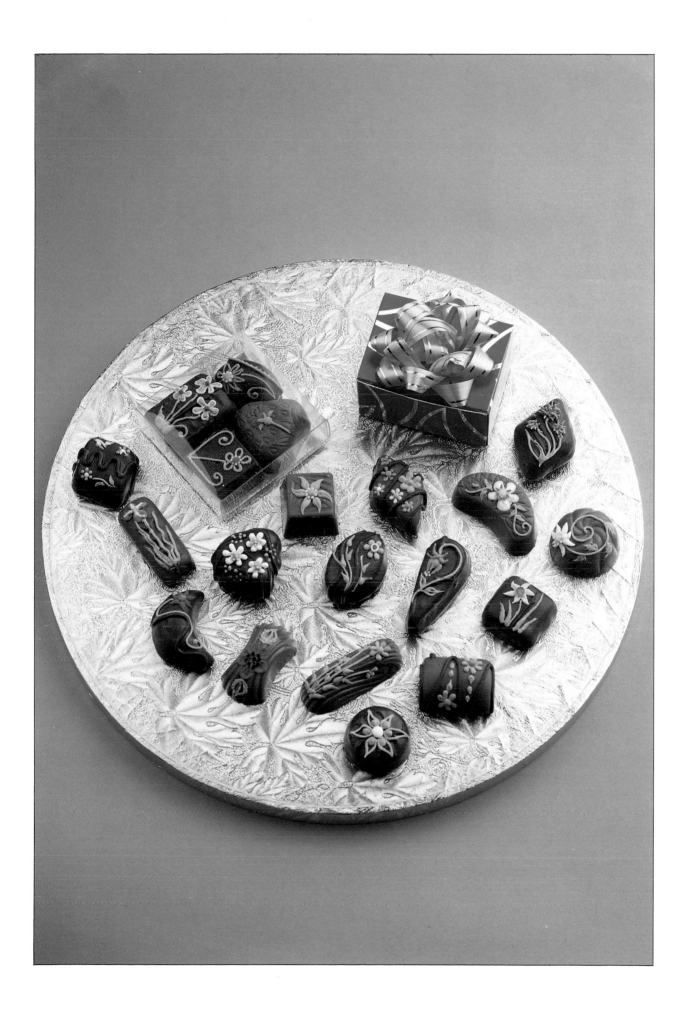

# CHOCOLATE LIQUEURS

**Ingredients**
prepared milk or plain
   chocolate cases (*see page 12*)
225g (8oz) granulated sugar
60ml (4 tbsp) cold water
30ml (2 tbsp) liqueur or spirit
melted plain or milk chocolate
   (*see page 10*)

1 Choose a selection of
attractive shapes of
chocolate cases, preferably
deep-moulded for the best
results.

2 Next make the liqueur
syrup. Place the sugar and
water in a small heavy-based
saucepan and bring to the boil
over a high heat to dissolve the
sugar. Boil the syrup to 108°C
(225°F) – transparent icing on
a sugar thermometer. Use a
pastry brush dipped in cold
water to brush down the inside
of the pan frequently to
prevent crystallization.
   Pour the mixture into a
measuring jug and stand this in
tepid water. Add ice cubes to
the water to bring down the
temperature. Add the liqueur
or spirit and shake gently to
mix. The syrup is ready to use
when cold.
   Using a small cream or milk
jug, pour the syrup into the
moulds leaving a small space at
the top of each so that a thin
film of chocolate can be
applied to seal the liqueur.
Leave in a cool place (not a
refrigerator) for 24 hours to
allow the surface to crystallize.

3 Using a small palette knife,
gently smooth a small
amount of melted chocolate
over the surface of each
chocolate liqueur to seal the
syrup. Leave to set.
   Everyone needs to be
warned before eating a
chocolate with a liquid filling,
so carefully wrap each variety
in different coloured foil which
will also serve to identify the
flavours easily. Pack in a sturdy
gift box to avoid damaging the
fragile chocolates.
NOTE   If using a liqueur with a
high sugar content, you will
need to reduce the amount of
sugar in the recipe – otherwise
the syrup will crystallize too
quickly. Do not be tempted to
add more than the amount of
liqueur given in the recipe.

# CHERRY WHIRLS

**Ingredients**
225g (8oz) cocktail cherries in
  maraschino, or glacé cherries
  and maraschino liqueur
melted plain or milk chocolate
  (*see page 10*)
crystallized rose petals (*see page
  27*)

1 If you decide to make your
  own liqueur-soaked fruit
rather than buy cocktail
cherries, prepare the fruit a few
days in advance to allow the
flavour to penetrate. Place the
glacé cherries (leave the coating
syrup on) in a screw-topped jar
or plastic container with air-
tight lid and pour over the
maraschino liqueur. Leave the
fruit to marinate gently,
shaking the container
occasionally to mix. Drain the
liqueur from the fruit and
stand the cherries on a piece of
absorbent kitchen paper ready
for use.

2 Prepare small chocolate
  drops by piping melted
chocolate on to waxed paper
with a greaseproof piping bag.
  When the drops are partly
set, place a liqueur-soaked
cherry on each – the chocolate
should hold the cherry in place
when fully set.

3 Turn the remaining
  chocolate left after
preparation of the centres into
piping or thickened chocolate.
Stir a few drops of cold water
into the chocolate, carefully
mixing after each drop. The
chocolate will gradually
become thicker making it ideal
for piping through a nozzle
and retaining its shape.
  Place a No42 nozzle in a
greaseproof paper piping bag
and three-quarters fill with the
thickened chocolate. Pipe a
whirl of chocolate over each
cherry centre, starting at the
base and winding round to the
top. Take care to cover the
whole cherry with chocolate to
seal it completely.
  While the chocolate is still
soft, place a tiny piece of
crystallized rose petal on each
whirl to give a simple, classic
finish to the chocolate. Place
the finished chocolates in paper
cases.

# PINEAPPLE KIRSCH CREAMS

## Ingredients
25ml (5 tsp) double (thick)
  dairy cream
90g (3oz) white chocolate,
  chopped
kirsch to taste
glacé pineapple (*see page 24*)
24 prepared white chocolate
  cases (*see page 10*)
melted white chocolate (*see page
  10*)
crystallized violets (*see page 27*)

1 Bring the cream to the boil
  in a saucepan. Remove from
the heat and add the chopped
chocolate. Continue stirring
until it has all melted and there
are no lumps. Stir in some
kirsch to taste and leave the
mixture to cool.

  Cut the glacé pineapple into
small pieces and place two or
three in each prepared case.

2 Fill a greaseproof paper
  piping bag with the cool
but not firm kirsch-flavoured
white ganache mixture. The
mixture should still be runny.
If the mixture has become too
firm, warm it gently over a
bowl of hot water, stirring
continuously. Pipe the mixture
into the white chocolate cases,
leaving just enough space to
smooth off the base. When
piping in the mixture, pipe into
all the spaces around the glacé
pineapple so that it becomes
completely sealed. Leave until
firm.

3 Using a little melted white
  chocolate and a small
palette knife, smooth off the
base of each piece. Leave to
set, then turn out the finished
chocolates from the moulds.
Decorate with small pieces of
crystallized violet.

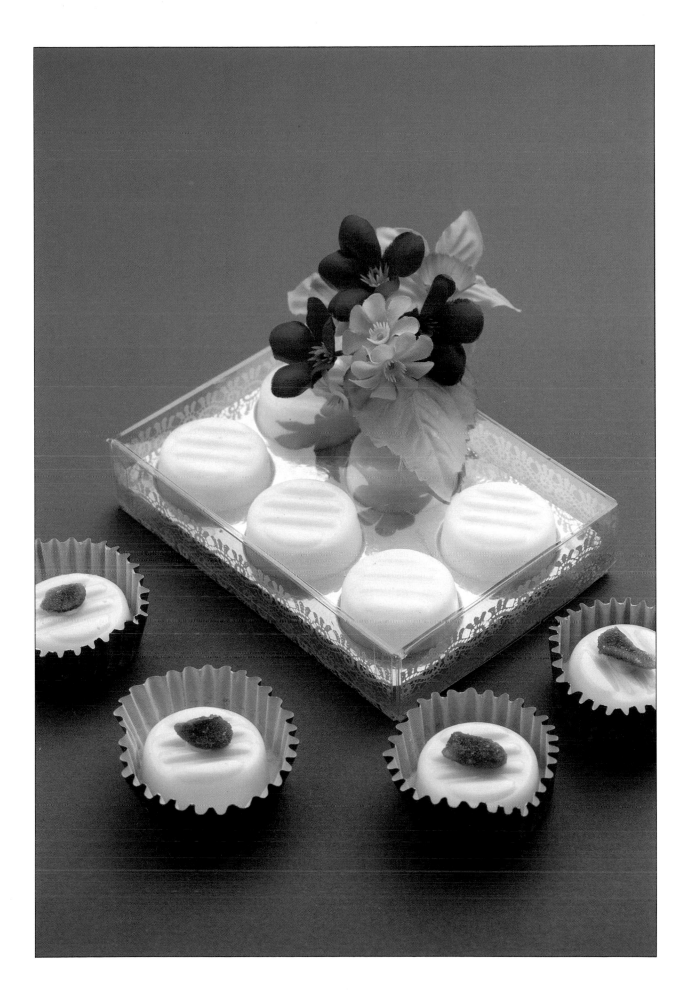

# CHERRY BRANDY CUPS

**Ingredients**
12 glacé cherries
brandy
25ml (5 tsp) double (thick)
  dairy cream
90g (3oz) milk chocolate,
  chopped
24 prepared plain chocolate
  cases (*see page 12*)
melted plain chocolate (*see page
  10*)

1 Place the cherries in a screw-topped jar or air-tight plastic container, pour the brandy over the fruit and leave to stand for about 12 hours, gently shaking the container occasionally.

2 Prepare the ganache filling. Bring the cream to the boil in a saucepan. Remove from the heat and add the chopped chocolate. Continue stirring until it has all melted and there are no lumps. Add some brandy to taste and stir in thoroughly. Leave the mixture to cool.

3 Drain the juice from the cherries and stand them on absorbent kitchen paper. Cut each cherry in half and place a half in each of the prepared chocolate cases. If you place the cherries in the cases with the rounded side facing downwards, they will fit better and be easier to finish.

4 Fill a greaseproof paper piping bag with the cooled but not firm ganache mixture. The mixture should be runny; if it has set too firmly, simply warm it over a bowl of hot water stirring constantly until the correct consistency is obtained.
  Pipe the ganache mixture into the chocolate cases filling in the spaces around the cherries to seal them and stopping just short of the top, thus enabling a thin coat of chocolate to be applied. Leave the ganache to become firm.

5 Using a small palette knife, smooth off the base of each chocolate with some melted chocolate. Leave to set. Then remove the chocolates from the moulds and place in paper cases ready for presentation.

6 Decorate the tops of the chocolates with red and green royal icing to make a cherry and leaf motif.

## Ingredients

45ml (3 tbsp) double (thick)
  dairy cream
10ml (2 tsp) instant coffee
  granules
175g (6oz) plain or milk
  chocolate, chopped
melted plain or milk chocolate
  for dipping (*see page 10*)
even-sized walnut pieces

1 Make the chocolate centres
first. Bring the cream to the
boil in a saucepan, add the
coffee granules and stir to
dissolve. Remove from the heat
and add the chopped chocolate.
Continue stirring until it has all
melted and there are no lumps.

Pour the mixture into a foil-
lined baking tray or special
sweet-making tray (*see page 12*).
To obtain the required depth
of filling using the recipe
given, the tray should measure
about 10 × 17.5-cm (4 ×
7-in). Leave the mixture to
cool and set fully, refrigerating
if necessary to quicken the
setting time.

2 When fully set, turn the
slab of mixture out of the
tray and trim all the edges with
a knife that has been dipped in
hot water and dried. Cut the
slab into pieces about 12-mm
× 2.5-cm ($\frac{1}{2}$ × 1-in). Place the
cut shapes on waxed paper
ready for dipping.

3 Using a dipping fork, dip
each centre into the melted
chocolate, allowing the excess
to drain away. Smooth the base
of the centre along the edge of
the chocolate pan or use a
palette knife. Place the
chocolates on waxed paper to
set. If 'feet' start to form
because too much chocolate
was left on the centres,
carefully slide each one along
the waxed paper, leaving
behind the excess chocolate.

Before the chocolate sets
fully, decorate each Supreme
with a neat piece of walnut.

# SPECIAL TRUFFLES

**Ingredients**
45ml (3 tbsp) double (thick) dairy cream
175g (6oz) milk, plain or white chocolate, chopped
30ml (2 tbsp) brandy for milk chocolate, or rum for plain chocolate, or kirsch or Champagne for white chocolate
icing (confectioner's) sugar for dusting
melted milk, plain or white chocolate for dipping (*see page 10*)

1 First make the filling for the centres. Bring the cream to the boil in a saucepan. Remove from the heat and add the chopped chocolate. Continue stirring until it has all melted and there are no lumps. Stir in the appropriate alcoholic flavouring and mix thoroughly. Pour the mixture into a shallow tray or plastic bowl and leave aside to cool completely. To quicken the process, you can chill the mixture in a refrigerator.

2 When the mixture is completely cool and firm, turn it out on to a work surface lightly dusted with icing sugar. Flatten the mixture using a rolling pin and your hands to make a pliable, plastic-type paste.

Roll the mixture into long sausage shapes, again using a little icing sugar. Cut into even-sized pieces as required.

Roll each portion lightly into a neat ball shape. The warmth from your hands will at this stage melt the chocolate a little. Place each rolled ball on waxed paper. The truffles could be rolled in chocolate vermicelli to make an attractive finish.

3 Using a dipping fork or skewer, dip each truffle into the melted chocolate (of the same type used for the centres), allowing any excess to drain away. Place the dipped centres on a wire rack and as the chocolate coating sets, roll the truffle along the wire rack to make a peaked textured finish as shown. Leave to set.

If the truffle centres are not completely covered with the first dipping, repeat the process. Place the finished truffles in paper cases ready for presentation.

# ALPINE BRANDY LOG

## Ingredients

175g (6oz) milk chocolate, chopped
45ml (3 tbsp) double (thick) dairy cream
30ml (2 tbsp) brandy
green-coloured marzipan
melted milk chocolate (*see page 10*)
icing (confectioner's) sugar

**1** First prepare the ganache filling. Bring the cream to the boil in a saucepan. Remove from the heat and add the chopped chocolate. Continue stirring until it has all melted and there are no lumps. Add the brandy and stir in thoroughly. Pour the mixture into a shallow tray or plastic bowl. Leave to cool and set.

Roll out the green-coloured marzipan into a long narrow strip, using a little icing sugar for dusting.

**2** Turn the ganache filling out of the container and make into a pliable, plastic-type mixture. Use a rolling pin and a little icing sugar dusting to soften the paste slightly. Roll out long sausage shapes and place along the edge of the green-coloured marzipan strip.

Wrap the green-coloured marzipan around the chocolate centre, trim off any excess marzipan and re-roll the log to neaten the shape.

**3** Place the log on a sheet of waxed paper and brush melted chocolate along the length, using a pastry brush, or texture the surface with a fork while still soft. Leave to set.

Cut the log into small pieces using a sharp knife dipped into hot water. Lightly dust the surface of each piece with icing sugar and then place in paper cases ready for packing.

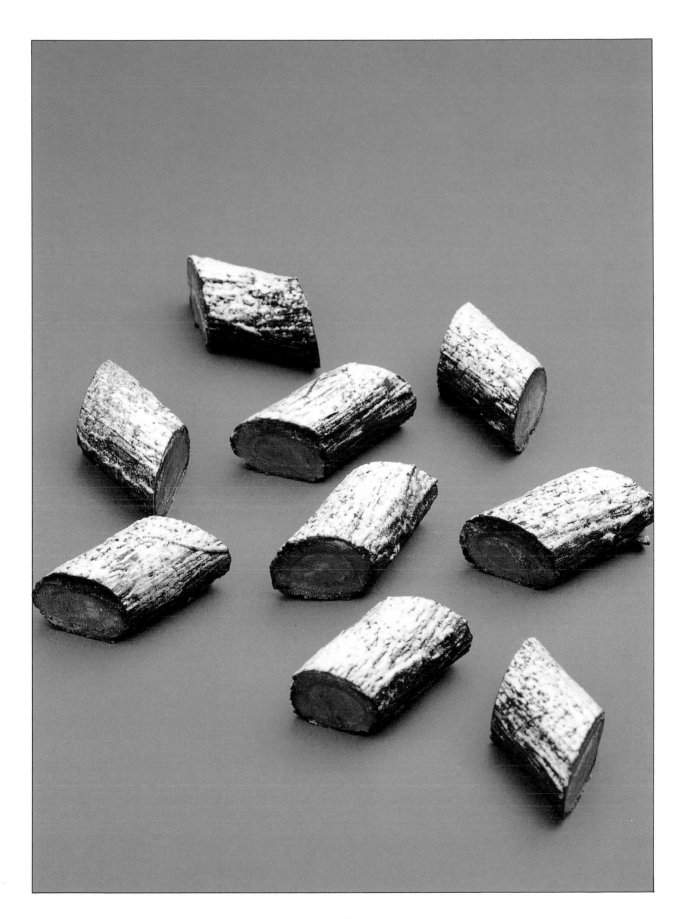

# GINGER CHRISTMAS TREE DECORATIONS

**Ingredients**
150g (5oz) butter
225g (8oz) plain (all-purpose)
  flour
125g (4oz) brown sugar
7g ($\frac{1}{4}$oz) ground ginger
pinch of baking powder
150g (5oz) golden syrup,
  slightly warmed
melted plain or milk chocolate
  (*see page 10*)
sugarpaste
marzipan
royal icing
assorted paste food colourings
  or food colour pens
egg white

1 Rub the butter through the
  dry ingredients to make a
fine crumble. Add the syrup
and mix to a smooth dough.
Leave in the refrigerator for
about 1 hour before using.

2 Roll out the biscuit dough
  to about 9mm (⅜-in)
thickness, dusting with a little
flour. Cut out round and oval
shapes with food cutters. Make
a small hole with a No4 nozzle
in each shape for the hanger.
Place the biscuits on a lightly
greased baking tray and bake at
190°C (370°F) Gas Mark 5 for
about 12 minutes or until
golden. Leave on the trays
until firm to the touch but not
completely cold, then transfer
to a wire rack and leave to
finish cooling.

3 When cool spread the base
  of each biscuit with melted
milk or plain chocolate and
leave on waxed paper until
quite set.

4 Colour some marzipan or
  sugarpaste in a variety of
different colours and use to
make various cut-out Christmas
faces such as Santa, snowmen
and angels. Attach the shapes
to the biscuits with a little
melted chocolate or royal icing.
Pipe the eyes on with white
and brown-coloured royal
icing.

  Alternatively, the biscuits
can be decorated with painted
Christmas scenes – these are
more suitable as gifts for
adults. Roll out some
sugarpaste thinly and cut to the
required shape. Spread a thin
layer of royal icing on each
biscuit and attach a sugarpaste
cut-out. Leave for a few hours
to become firm.

  Use edible food colourings
and a fine paint brush or edible
food colour pens to paint your
favourite Christmas scenes.
Many ideas can be gleaned
from gift wrapping paper and
Christmas cards.

  When the biscuits are
decorated, you can thread some
gold or silver gift tie through
the hole in each one to enable
you to hang them on your
Christmas tree.

# FLORENTINES

### Ingredients
50g (2oz) butter
50g (2oz) brown sugar
5ml (1 tsp) honey
15ml (1 tbsp) chopped walnuts
15ml (1 tbsp) nibbed or
  chopped flaked almonds
15ml (1 tbsp) chopped glacé
  cherries
5ml (1 tsp) chopped glacé
  ginger
5ml (1 tsp) evaporated milk
5ml (1 tsp) plain (all-purpose)
  flour
melted milk, plain or white
  chocolate (*see page 10*)

1 Melt the butter in a
  saucepan, add the sugar and
honey and bring to the boil.
Remove from the heat.

Stir in the prepared nuts,
cherries and ginger, then add
the evaporated milk and lastly
the flour. Lightly grease a
miniature bun tin (pan) with
butter or margarine. Using a
teaspoon, place small amounts
of the florentine mixture in
each indent. Bake the
florentines at 190°C (375°F)
Gas Mark 5 for 8–9 minutes or
until golden brown.

Leave the florentines in the
bun tin for a short time until
they start to set and become
firm. You can neaten the edges
with a small knife while the
caramel is setting. When
slightly cool, remove the
florentines from the tin, using
a small knife to release them,
and place on waxed paper
ready for decoration. If you
should leave the florentines in
the tin too long and they stick,
just warm them slightly in the
oven to release them.

2 Spread some melted
  chocolate on waxed paper,
smoothing out with a cranked
palette knife. Shake the paper a
little to assist the flow of the
chocolate and to obtain a flat
surface. Leave to set.

Pour some more melted
chocolate over the previously
prepared chocolate and while
still soft, use a comb scraper to
create a wavy pattern on the
chocolate. Move the scraper
from side to side along the
chocolate in a smooth flowing
action. Leave to set.

3 Using a small round food
  cutter the same diameter as
the florentines, cut out a
matching number of discs of
chocolate. Brush a little melted
chocolate on the flat side of
each florentine and attach the
prepared discs. You can spread
and texture the chocolate
directly on to the florentine but
the recommended way is far
easier and looks neater when
finished.

Package a selection of milk,
plain and white chocolate
decorated florentines – they
make a welcome gift or a super
tea-time treat!

# CAKE TRUFFLES

**Ingredients**

275g (10oz) plain or chocolate
  cake crumbs
50g (2oz) ground almonds
25g (1oz) apricot jam
60ml (4 tbsp) evaporated milk
50–90g (2–3oz) plain chocolate,
  melted
icing (confectioner's) sugar for
  dusting
melted plain and milk chocolate
  for dipping (*see page 10*)
plain and milk chocolate
  vermicelli
chocolate shavings
roasted flaked almonds
cocoa powder

1 Mix the cake crumbs and
ground almonds together
and then add the jam,
evaporated milk and chocolate,
mixing thoroughly to a firm
paste. The amount of chocolate
required depends upon the
moisture content of your cake
crumbs. Chill for 30 minutes
before use.

2 Roll the mixture out into a
long sausage shape and cut
into small pieces. Roll half of
the pieces into neat round balls
and the other half into small
finger shapes. Use a little icing
sugar for dusting to prevent
the mixture from sticking to
the work surface.

3 Prepare your work area so
that the finishing off runs in
a smooth logical sequence.
Have ready your prepared
truffle centres, the dipping
chocolate. followed by the
masking material and finally a
sheet of waxed paper to place
the finished truffles on. You
could even place the truffles
directly in the paper cases if
they do not require any further
decoration.

4 At this stage it is best to
have some assistance from
another person to roll the
chocolate-coated truffles in the
chosen masking material as
your hands will be covered
with melted chocolate. Take a
small amount of melted
chocolate in the palm of both
hands and roll each truffle
gently in your hands to cover
with a thin film of chocolate.

Place the coated truffle in the
masking material and ask your
helper to roll the truffle and
completely cover it in masking
material. The truffles are then
left on waxed paper to set
fully.

The truffles may be left as
they are or can be further
decorated by lightly dusting
with icing sugar, using a tea
strainer or very fine sieve. A
fine dusting of equal parts of
icing sugar and cocoa powder
mixed together makes a nice
finish on truffles that have just
been rolled in chocolate and
not actually masked. Place the
truffles in paper cases.

# FANCY CAKES

**Ingredients**
apricot jam
fancy cakes baked in small bun
   tins (pans)
glacé icing
instant coffee granules
melted chocolate (*see page 10*)
assorted food colourings
buttercream
selection of decorations, nuts
   and glacé fruits

1 Boil the apricot jam in a
saucepan (adding a little
water to thin if necessary) and
using a pastry brush, lightly
brush the jam over the top of
each cake to the edges. This
not only seals the cake,
therefore keeping it fresher for
a longer period, but also adds
another flavour.

2 Divide the cakes into six
separate batches ready for
the different colours of icing.
Warm some white glacé icing
over a pan of hot water and
use to ice the tops of one
batch. Use a small palette knife
and take the icing to just short
of the edges to allow for a
little flow.
   Divide the remaining glacé
icing and keep it warm over
bowls or pans of hot water.
Colour one half lemon and one
half pink and use to ice the
tops of two more batches.
Then mix the two colours of
glacé icing together to make
pale orange, adding more
orange food colouring if
required. Ice another batch.
For the last two batches add a
little instant coffee dissolved in
hot water and use to ice one
batch. Then stir in some
melted chocolate to make
chocolate icing for the
remaining cakes.

3 Using buttercream, pipe the
designs as shown on the
cakes and decorate as liked.

# FRUITY CRUNCHIES

**Ingredients**
equal quantities of:
  chopped walnuts
  chopped hazelnuts
  flaked almonds
  sultanas
  glacé cherries
  cornflakes
melted white chocolate (*see page 10*)
melted plain chocolate (*see page 10*)

1 Set out some small paper cases ready for the mixture.

2 Place all the nuts and fruits in a large bowl and stand it over a pan of hot water. Add the cornflakes and sufficient melted white chocolate to bind all the ingredients to a dropping consistency.
  Using a teaspoon, pile small amounts of the mixture high in the paper cases, keeping the texture rough. Leave to set.

3 Use scissors to snip off the end of a small greaseproof paper piping bag filled with melted plain chocolate. With a short side-to-side movement spin some fine lines of chocolate over the crunchies. Leave to set.

# LITTLE CHRISTMAS PUDDINGS

**Ingredients**
300g (10oz) plain or chocolate
   sponge cake crumbs
25g (1oz) ground almonds
25g (1oz) apricot jam
60ml (4 fl oz) evaporated milk
30ml (2 tbsp) rum
5ml (1 tsp) chopped walnuts
5ml (1 tsp) chopped glacé
   cherries
5ml (1 tsp) chopped glacé
   ginger
5ml (1 tsp) chopped sultanas
about 50g (2oz) melted
   chocolate (*see page 10*)
icing (confectioner's) sugar for
   dusting
natural marzipan or white
   sugarpaste
melted plain chocolate (*see page
   10*)
pouring fondant or glacé icing
egg-yellow paste food
   colouring
green-coloured royal icing
red-coloured royal icing

1 Mix the cake crumbs and
   ground almonds together,
then add the other ingredients
and mix well to a firm paste.
The amount of chocolate
required depends upon the
moisture content of your
sponge cake crumbs. Chill for
30 minutes before use.
   Roll the mixture into a long
sausage shape, using a little
icing sugar for dusting. Cut
into even-sized pieces, then roll
each one into a neat ball shape
and place on waxed paper.

2 Prepare the plates for the
   puddings by rolling out
some marzipan or sugarpaste
thinly and cutting out some
small fluted circles. Place the
circles in small bun tins (pans)
or plastic fruit trays to dry in a
curved shape.

3 Using a dipping fork or
   skewer, dip each centre into
the melted chocolate allowing
any excess to drain away. Place
each dipped ball on a prepared
plate. Leave to set.

4 Warm the pouring fondant
   or glacé icing in a double
jacketed pan and colour egg-
yellow. Using a small
greaseproof paper piping bag
with a small hole cut at one
end, pipe a little of the icing
on top of each pudding to
represent custard, allowing
some to run down the side.

5 Fit No2 nozzles in two
   small greaseproof paper
piping bags and half-fill with
green- and red-coloured royal
icing respectively. Pipe three
small 'spikes' for holly leaves
on each pudding and three red
berries.

# CRISPY CHOIRBOYS

**Ingredients**
puffed rice cereal
melted milk or plain chocolate
   (*see page 10*)
marzipan
white sugarpaste or flower
   paste
red, flesh, egg-yellow, brown
   and black paste food
   colourings
royal icing
rice paper

1 Place the puffed rice cereal in a bowl over hot water and mix in sufficient melted chocolate to cover the cereal and bind together.

Lay a sheet of waxed paper on a cake board and arrange 4-cm (1¾-in) diameter food cutters on top. Line each food cutter with a narrow strip of waxed paper.

2 To make the body shapes, fill the chocolate and cereal mixture into the lined cutters using a teaspoon. Flatten the top smoothly with the back of the spoon. Leave to set before removing the shapes from the cutters.

Pipe some chocolate discs or large drops on to waxed paper and leave to set. Attach a prepared body shape to each disc with a little melted chocolate, supporting if necessary until set.

3 Colour some marzipan with red paste food colouring for the arms and roll out into a sausage shape. Cut to length and attach to the body with a little melted chocolate. Next cut out a small fluted circle of thinly rolled white sugarpaste and attach, to form the ruffle. Make a small depression for the head in the centre of the ruffle with a modelling tool or your thumb.

Roll a small oval shape in flesh-coloured marzipan for the head and indent the eyes with a modelling tool or end of a paint brush. Attach a tiny ball of flesh-coloured marzipan for the nose with egg white. Press on a tiny ball of red-coloured marzipan for the mouth, with the end of a paint brush, moving it up and down to make a long oval mouth giving the impression of a choirboy reaching a high note. Attach the head to the ruffle on the body with white royal icing.

Pipe the eyes with white royal icing and a No2 nozzle and overpipe with brown-coloured royal icing. Pipe the hair on with egg-yellow-, brown- or black-coloured royal icing using a No1 nozzle to pull up spikes as shown. The face can be tinted with petal dust or sprayed with an airbrush using pinky-orange colour to create a complexion.

4 Cover the choirboys in cellophane tied with an attractive ribbon and bow and gift tag. Alternatively, present them singly or in groups in boxes. They also make original party place settings especially when further decorated with a name or inscription plaque in sugarpaste.

# LOLLY FACES

**Ingredients**
packet of assorted fruit-
    flavoured and toffee lollies
royal icing
marzipan
sugarpaste
egg white
assorted paste food colourings

1 Unwrap the lollies and press
the sticks into a block of
polystyrene foam to make
working on them easier.

2 You can be really creative
with these novelty faces so
colour the marzipan and
sugarpaste in bright attractive
colours that young children
will appreciate.
   Hats are easily made from
semi-circles, balls or strips of
marzipan as shown. Attach the
brims of the hats with a little
egg white and then decorate
them with badges or flowers.
   Miniature plaits of hair can
be formed from strips of
marzipan. You could also press
coloured marzipan through a
tea strainer or clay gun to
create a good effect. Attach the
hair to the lollies with a little
royal icing.
   Bow-ties are quick to make
from thinly rolled-out
sugarpaste cut into small
triangular shapes and attached
together with a tiny ball of
sugarpaste and some egg white.
Spotted bow ties are made by
pressing tiny balls of coloured
sugarpaste in the rolled-out
paste at the first stage.

3 Pipe eyes on the faces in
white royal icing with a
No2 nozzle, then overpipe with
brown. Noses, mouths and ears
are made from marzipan and
attached with tiny dabs of royal
icing.
   The finished lollies can be
wrapped in cellophane and tied
with an attractive bow and gift
tag.

# SHORTBREAD SETTINGS

**Ingredients**
packet of round shortbread
   biscuits
melted chocolate (*see page 10*)
sugarpaste
marzipan (optional)
icing (confectioner's) sugar for
   dusting
flower paste (optional)
assorted paste food colourings
royal icing
non-pareils

1 Spread the back of each
shortbread biscuit with
melted chocolate. This gives
them more stability for
handling and also introduces
another texture and delicious
flavour. Place the biscuits on
waxed paper and leave to set.

2 Colour some sugarpaste or
marzipan and roll out quite
thinly, using a little icing sugar
for dusting. Using a fluted
cutter the size of the biscuit cut
out a disc for each biscuit.
   Attach the sugarpaste or
marzipan discs to the biscuits
with royal icing. Leave to set.

3 Roll out some sugarpaste
(or use flower paste) of a
different colour thinly. Using
plunger or flower cutters,
stamp out flower shapes. Place
on clean foam sponge, pressing
lightly in the centre to make a
depression. Leave to set. Also
cut out some green-coloured
leaves.
   Pipe a bulb of royal icing in
the centre of each flower and
lightly press into coloured non-
pareils.
   Attach the flowers and
leaves to the prepared biscuit
bases, using a little royal icing.
To complete the place settings,
pipe the guest's name in
coloured royal icing, using a
No1 nozzle.

# PRESENTATION AND PACKAGING

After spending a considerable time producing your delicious hand-made sweets and treats, it is worthwhile devoting just as much thought to their packaging and presentation. Give your sweets and treats that individual look, that personalized touch, that extra special something!

Beautifully presented home-made sweets make ideal gifts, showing you care enough about the recipients to spend time creating attractive packaging.

You can buy small gift boxes, gift tags and novelty bags from stationers, sugarcraft suppliers and greeting card shops. Paper and foil cases can also be purchased from the same places.

Truffles (*see page 41*) can be packed in a gift box and decorated with a shiny ribbon and bow – add a special touch with some tiny silk flowers.

A transparent heart-shaped box decorated with a miniature bouquet of flowers is ideal for Valentine's Day, engagement or wedding receptions as take-home gifts for the guests.

Make your own chocolate box, using a commercially available mould. Pipe a decorative edging in royal icing and pack your chocolates inside.

Small paper or foil gift bags look wonderful packed with Fruity Crunchies (*see page 52*) or Truffles (*see page 41*). Tie with a matching ribbon, bow and gift tag.

Keep the contents a surprise, pack the chocolates inside and tie with a ribbon and bow. Edible flowers make an extra special feature.

Cover half a cabbage with decorative foil gift wrapping paper and stick lots of Lolly Faces (*see page 58*) into it to make a super table centrepiece for a children's tea party.

Tiny boxes which hold one or two small chocolates (*see page 41*) or truffles (*see page 41*) make attractive party place settings or take-home gifts – or can even be used as Christmas tree decorations.

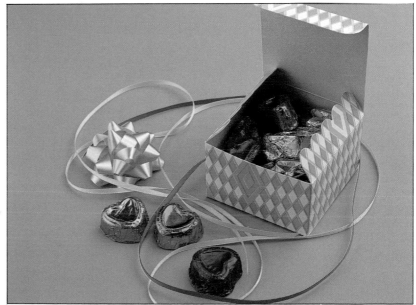

# PIPED CHOCOLATE DECORATIONS

**Ingredients**

melted milk, plain or white
  chocolate (*see page 10*)
water or glycerine

1 Prepare templates of the
  designs to be used. Trace
the patterns provided on to
white cartridge paper. Also cut
out small sheets of waxed
paper the same size as the
templates.

2 Prepare the melted
  chocolate for piping. For
this purpose you need to

thicken the chocolate. Add a
few drops of water or
glycerine, stirring gently after
each addition. After a few
additions the chocolate will
start to thicken, do not add *too
much* liquid as this would make
the chocolate too thick for
piping. Keep the chocolate
over a bowl of warm water.

  Half-fill a small greaseproof
paper piping bag with the
chocolate mixture and use
scissors to cut a neat hole at
the end of the bag about the
size of a No2 nozzle.

3 Place pieces of waxed paper
  over the templates and pipe
as for royal icing, following the
outlines carefully and neatly.
Avoid shaking the paper, as
this will make the chocolate
run. Place the piped pieces on
a cake board to finish setting,
which does not take long.

4 Small crystallized petals or
  coloured dragees make
interesting alternative finishes.
Peel the piped shapes off the
waxed paper and store ready to
use between sheets of waxed
paper. Alternatively, you can
pack the shapes in gift boxes to
give to your friends. Piped
chocolate shapes make lovely
decorations for special desserts,
ice creams, soufflés, cheesecakes
and many small cakes and
gâteaux.

*Examples of piped
chocolate decorations can be seen
on the cover of this book.*

PRINTED IN BELGIUM BY
proost
INTERNATIONAL BOOK PRODUCTION